Hup Pups

Written by Joanne Reay

Illustrated by Anne Kennedy

With a rum tum tum,
Hup Pup Drum.

Hup! Hup! Run!
Hup Pup Drum.

With a slug in a mug,
Hup Pup Bug.

Jump, Hup Pup Bug!

Rub-a-dub-dub,
Hup Pup Tub.

Jump, Hup Pup Tub!

All fluff and fuzz,
Hup Pup Buzz.

Jump, Hup Pup Buzz!

Yum, yum, yum!
Hup Pup Tum.

No! Don't jump, Hup Pup Tum!

Bump, bump, bump!
Thump, thump, thump!

Here are the Hup Pups all in a lump.

Can you find Drum, Bug, Tub, Buzz, and Tum?